To begin with, all boats were simple wooden dugouts with paddles.

The dugouts looked like this.

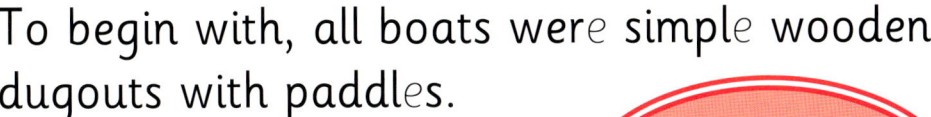

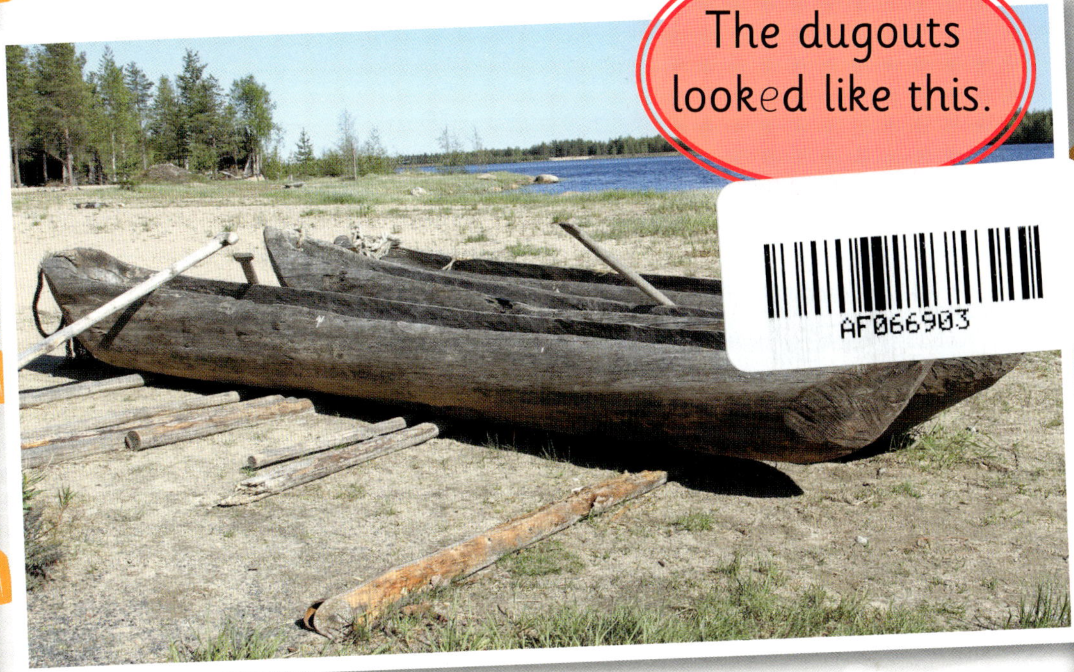

A dugout is made from a tree trunk. The middle is carved out, and then the outside is shaped to make the boat travel smoothly along the river.

Modern sailing boats have a lot more parts than a dugout.

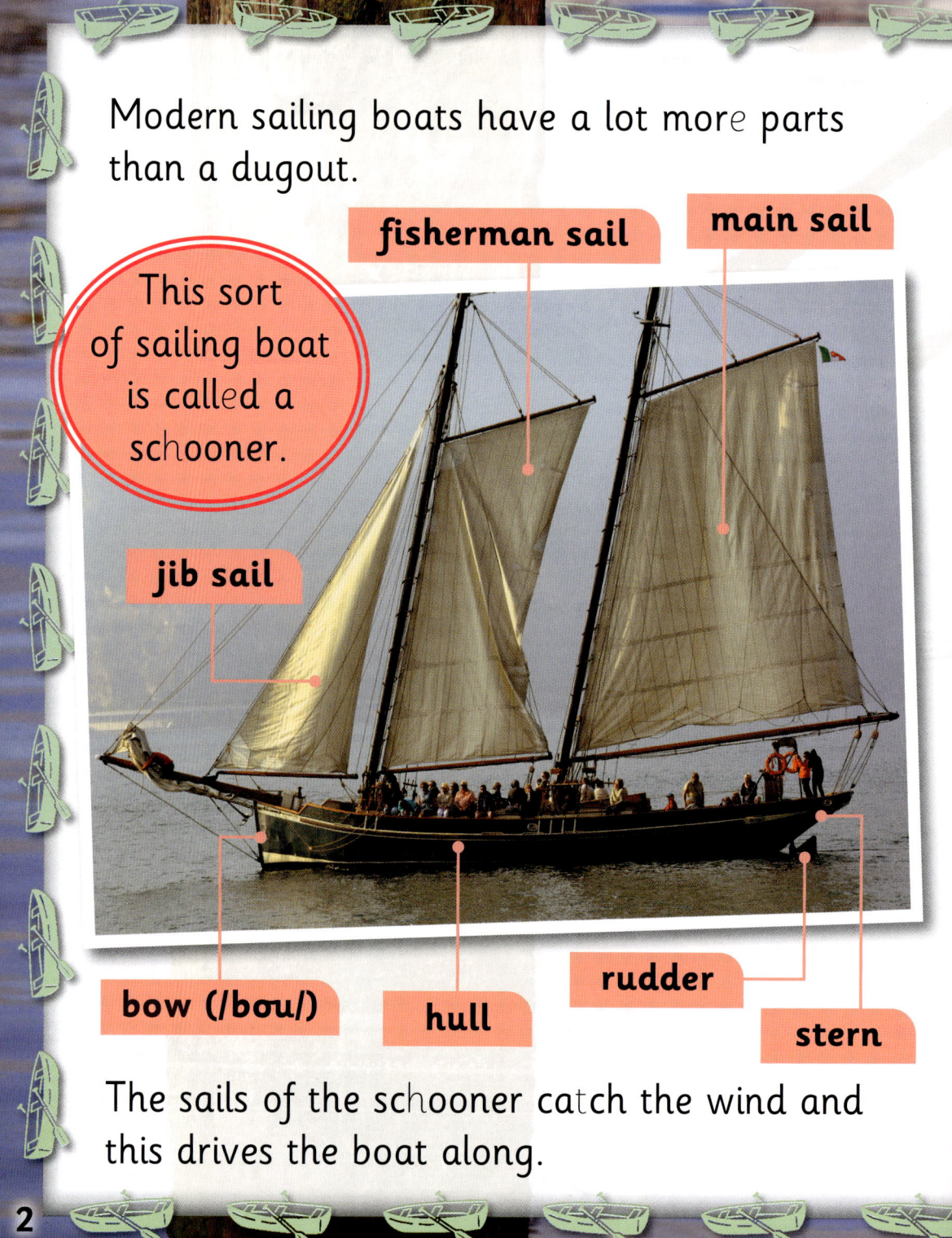

fisherman sail

main sail

This sort of sailing boat is called a schooner.

jib sail

bow (/boʊ/)

hull

rudder

stern

The sails of the schooner catch the wind and this drives the boat along.

But not all boats have sails.

Some boats have paddles or oars, which are used to paddle the boat along…

paddle

o**a**r

…while some boats, like this dinghy, have an engine (/**en**jin/) to make the boat go.

These boats have an outrigger. An outrigger is a long, thin float attached to the side of the boat by poles. It helps to stop the boat flipping over in strong waves.

outrigger

This boat has two outriggers.

As you can see, there are lots of different sorts of boats. Boats can be used for travelling, transporting goods, sports and fishing. Some boats are even used as homes!

travel

transporting goods

fishing

a home

A ferry is a big, tall boat that is used to take travellers on trips.

This ferry has three decks.

A ferry often has one or more lifeboats attached to the back or sides.

lifeboats

If a boat gets into trouble or starts to capsize (flip over) and sink, lifeboats are used to rescue everyone on board.

Lifeboats are kept by the coast and on the banks of big rivers as well as on ships.

The coastguard uses lifeboats like these to rescue struggling swimmers.

A lot of the things we buy are not made where we live. Container ships are used to bring goods (such as laptops, tablets and books) from where they were made to where they will be sold.

The shipping containers have all sorts of things inside. Even the book (or tablet) you are holding was shipped in a container like this!

Tugboats are strong little boats. They drag container ships and bigger boats into a port or along a canal.

tugboat

The tugboat is attached by a rope to the big ship.

A lot of boats are used for fishing. Bigger fishing boats tend to have nets on the sides or at the back. They catch fish as they drag the nets along.

Smaller, simpler boats are used for fishing, too. The fishermen catch the fish with rods and lines.

Some Japanese and Chinese (/**Chie**neez/) fishermen even use trained cormorants to help them to catch fish!

This is a cormorant.

The cormorant has a loose ring around its throat to stop it gobbling up all of the big fish, but it can still gobble up the smaller fish.

Houseboats are floating homes. They are quite common on canals, rivers and lakes.

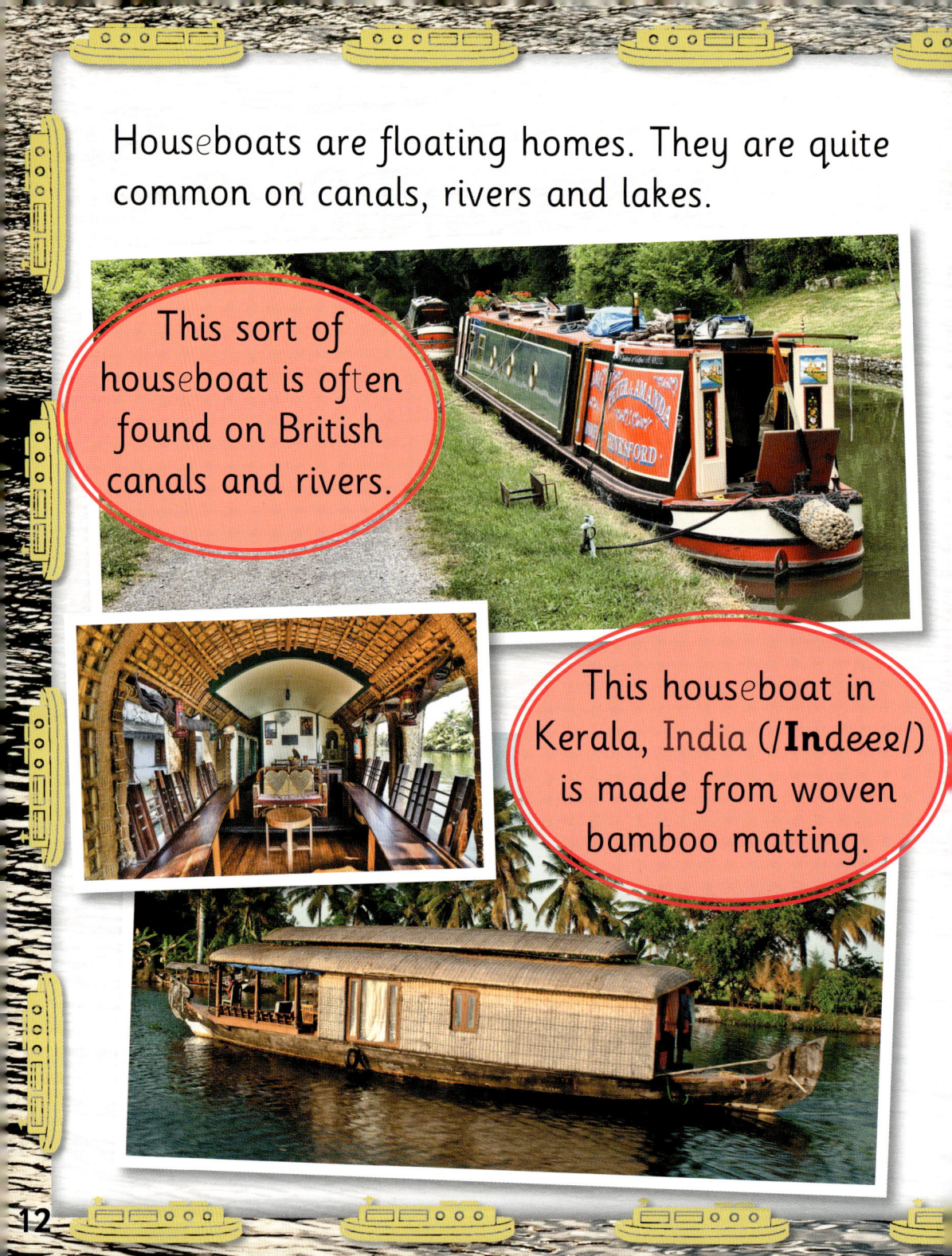

This sort of houseboat is often found on British canals and rivers.

This houseboat in Kerala, India (/**In**deeɹ/) is made from woven bamboo matting.

These boats are used in floating markets.

This floating market in Bangkok sells all sorts of different things, such as paintings, hats, food and silk.

Speedboats are used for sport and for fun.

Speedboats normally travel at up to 100mph (a hundred miles per hour), but the quickest speedboat ever recorded went at 317mph!

Some boats look a little different.

Normally, boats have one hull, but a catamaran has twin hulls, side by side.

catamaran

pontoon

Pontoons are flat, rectangle-shaped boats with floats. They are perfect for use on lakes and rivers, but not very safe when it is windy, or when the waves are big and choppy.

Tips for keeping safe on a boat

life jacket

1. Life jackets are a must!

2. If you fall in, lie floating on your back with your arms and legs outstretched. Then raise an arm and shout for help.

3. If someone else falls in, **do not** get in as well. Instead, toss them a life ring and drag them out.

This is a life ring attached to a rope.